LEGACY

Legacy

By Richard Harteis

Copyright©2007 by Richard Harteis
http://stores.lulu.com/TheChurchofLivingHopeBookstore

Copyright©2007 by Richard Harteis

All rights reserved, including the right to reproduce this book or portions thereof in any form whatsoever.

ISBN: 978-0-6151-6572-1
Library of Congress Catalog Card information pending

The following poems were first published in OCHO Magazine Issue #12 – September 2007 Guest Edited by Grace Cavalieri.
After the Rain
Memorial Day, 2007
Death and Taxes
In Memoriam, May 30, 2007
Evensong
Sentimental Reveille
Pathetic Fallacy

The author wishes to express his deep gratitude to Mary Buckley Parriott whose support has made the publication of LEGACY possible and to Dave and Jen Halliday for their advice and help in the production of the book. The author also wishes to thank David Woodward for his interest and technical support. A very special thanks to Grace Cavalieri for her love and encouragement.

Cover illustration: "What I Remember the Writer's Telling Me When I Was Young" from ECHOES, an art folio, book which contains poems by William Meredith and Richard Harteis with twelve Illustrations by Stoimen Stoilov (For information contact Riverrunbooks@cs.com or www.TheChurchofLivingHope.com)
A feature article on William Meredith's life and work can be found at http://drunkenboat.com/db7/feature-meredith/index.html#

Copies of LEGACY can be purchased at:
http://stores.lulu.com/TheChurchofLivingHopeBookstore

For William
our threads
invisible
but holding

Contents

ii.	Forward
1.	Last Songs for William
	I. Memorial Day, 2007
	II. Death and Taxes
	III. Evensong
	IV. In Memoriam, May 30, 2007
	V. Sentimental Reveille
6.	Homework
7.	Adrift
9.	Pathetic Fallacy*
11.	After the Rain
12.	The Deer are after the Apples again
13.	Counsel
15.	Apology
17.	Vin Triste
19.	Gardening
21.	Prayer to Cloacina *
22.	Aubade
23.	Quandary
24.	Moot Epiphany
25.	After Berry Picking
26.	Procrastination
27.	Vortex Ring State
28.	Mitzvah
30.	A Plan
32.	Can You Hear Me Now?
33.	Praying with Tammy Faye

35.	The Chinese Beech
37.	Flight Crew
39.	Veteran
40.	The Revenant
42.	A Full Year Come and Gone
44.	Post Card from Achill Island
45.	Solitary Confinement
47.	The Lesson
49.	Phylactery
51.	Symbiosis
53.	Day Tripper
56.	MacDowell Colony - Ireland West
58.	Spiderman
61.	Legacy

Foreword

In her remarkable book, THE YEAR OF MAGICAL THINKING, Joan Didion describes the grief one experiences when one loses a loved one, in her case both her husband and only child in the same tragic year. Grief, it turns out is another country, far different from anything one could have imagined. One's expectations and those of family friends do not include the vortex one is drawn into, the emotional collapse that sometimes occurs out of the blue as you walk down the street on a beautiful day or begin to prepare your dinner, alone. The constant presence of the loved one's absence threatens to destroy joy forever - the funeral is the easy part. This void in our lives may never abate. You may never really be able to "move on," or "get over it." Time may not, in fact, heal all wounds and life becomes a question of learning to live with loss, "the relentless succession of moments during which we will confront the experience of meaninglessness itself."
Iris Murdoch has described such moments of suffering as "black absolutes." And yet, she says, "Fortunate are those for whom these black stars shed some sort of light." They can help guide us as we try to cross the gulf of our grief, or as William Meredith has said of life's challenges in another context:

".... engage in the often friendless struggle. A long war, a pygmy war in ways, But island by island we must go across."

Last Songs for William

I. Memorial Day, 2007

I sit like a god
in the hospital penthouse
watching the crows
on the lower roof top
taking their supper -
old french fries, pilfered
from a dumpster, AC run off,
and stagnant rainwater.

All the bright day long,
ferries glide back and forth
to the islands. The nation
takes its pleasures: burgers
and chicken on the grill,
long walks, hand in hand,
a game of golf or tennis,
and remember a little
their dead. I sit alone with
my dying lover contemplating
hospice decisions, what to hold
what to give, like a Greek boy
whose need to rip the wings from flies
can not fully be explained.

II. Death and Taxes

two sure things,
both a certainty tonight.
April 15 has come and gone,
the IRS will surely call.
And as my darling lies sleeping
he turns his head from
time to time to the electrical storm
lighting up his dreams:

"You sulphurous and thought -executing fires,
Vaunt couriers of oak-cleaving thunderbolts,
Singe my white head! And thou, all shaking Thunder,
Strike flat the thick rotundity o' the world!"

Down the hall, a man heaves and
heaves, nothing left, can not empty
himself into the night. As I keep late watch
once again: time it seems, no longer on our side.

A dark figure, stands at the door,
his hand outstretched. "Pay up ,
young Yankee, come along.
And you may yet get out alive."

III. Evensong

This bronze angel against the grey of evening,
wreaths in hand, like tambourines to celebrate
your own genius, that balance, that talent
to stand on a ball fire, grow trees,
love profoundly, inspire: model of
civility, the ultimate good guy.

Now your blue eyes grow grey
with the fading of the light.
You breathe steadily into the blue
oxygen mask, preparing for lift off.
What adventure awaits you? This
private mission we all must undertake.
Do I ask you to look out for me from
the stars as you have done all these years?
I know you will, I know I needn't ask.

I'll keep the angel though,
I'll hold her hostage to keep
your memory safe here on earth
where we have known you
and will love you
until it is time
myself to take flight.

IV. In Memoriam, May 30, 2007

The moon was full, the evening cool,
a perfect night for dying. We packed up
our room and had Irish whiskey with friends
into the night. I knew that was the last time
I would ever see you in life, growing cold
under my touch. I kissed your lips, made
the fish "o" they had become, and took in
from your lungs the last breath. And gave
you mine. And your words come back:

"I think dear one that one day I'll fall off
this galaxy, leaving husk and canvas behind,
the loneliness I'll take with me made whole,
myself made whole, by what we've said
in these knocking moments, oh,
and keeping, as hearts keep
(husks and canvas being little abandoned houses),
and going away so."

And the loneliness I am left with is made whole
too my dear by what we've said and been for
each other all these long years. But, oh, oh,
I seem already to be lost in the cold skin
of the globe, aching for the moon.

V. Sentimental Reveille

Each day begins the same:
"Where are you my love?"
The terrible fact - you are no more,
are not lying still asleep beside me,
not the sweet echo, as I call the dog
to join us in bed to lick your nose,
to start the day, each startling
morning now without you.

She cocks her head
and licks instead my tears.

A penguin, a white wolf
take shape in the crumpled
tissues on the night stand,
affirm the dull irony:

When the sun pours into my sleep
And I first open my eyes, you
are never to be seen again,
but in dream.

Homework

The manuals describe
four responses to tragedy:
1. Stoicism
2. Martyrdom
3. Suicide
4. Transformation

Who wouldn't go for
door number four?

"Good memories
pushing us forward."

"All life is on loan."

"The demons of self-pity
and discouragement
drag us into darkness."

All true, all true.
But he will never come back
nor I, nor you.

I lay the book aside
and weep.

Adrift

Afraid I may actually die
of a broken heart, I visit
the local ER for an EKG,
CPK levels for an old MI,
an MRI, a CT or PET scan:
an alphabet soup when you're
out of sorts body and soul,
some chicken broth when
you're feeling chicken, a little
TLC, the occasional PDA.

Decisiveness is manliness as
Marie Antoinette discovered
with the price of her head, but
I'm a Jackson Pollack portrait
of indecision, a textbook mess.

"Get back, get back, get back
to where you want to belong,"
as the Beatles sang. Cher should
stomp into my kitchen and
slap me up the side of my head:
"Snap out of it!" But how to get
your mojo back? "Are you happy," I asked the

peanut princess who floated
up to William in his wheel chair
as we strolled one evening at
flamingo hour in West Palm Beach.
"What's not to like," said the young
divorcee, sipping her mojito martini.
"I live in this palace, I shop every day.
Look at this belt," she said, twirling
around her tight little blue-jeaned
butt. "It cost two thousand dollars!"

"But are you lonely," I ask.

"I've got 'Sir lance a lot'," she laughs,
her electric charger. She's not interested
in a toy boy. She's after the old boy I've
bailed out of the nursing home. It's
his eyes and beautiful smile she's after
that no longer ever will light my life again
as pink clouds take flight in the evening sky.

Pathetic Fallacy*

Rain at last this summer morning
when day after day the relentless sun
burned the land, a blanket of heat
heavy as grief, the sweltering dream
I've lived in since your death.

Each morning the particulars
overwhelm me, each night
I take your ghost to bed.

I wear a sunburst on my shoulder,
you, a crescent moon and star -
cliché symbols the tattoo artist
thought cute in two guys 60 and 88.

I burn on alone, out of balance
as cardinals play in the summer rain.

"He'll have to live with it," the doctor said
when I asked for something to relieve
your nightmares. "No, no. No antibiotics
for the swollen eye. The eye drops will do."
I'd like to carve his words into the sky,
write them on the walls with my blood.

But the world I guess has enough
proof of man's potential for cruelty.

I stare at the small bottle on my desk:
Akwa Tears, 15 ml, disp: 05/25/07.
The bottle is almost full, but
your eyes are closed forever now,
and I have no need of artificial tears.

* Pathetic Fallacy: endowing inanimate, natural objects with human feelings, e.g. The sky is weeping

After the Rain

For decades I tended to
the details of your life:
bathing, cooking,
filling the pill box
doing the laundry -
soup to nuts.

Tonight, at my leisure
I sit alone on the point
in awe as the Thames dissolves
into a Chinese landscape,
the delicate fog, a grey curtain
erasing the horizon
obscuring the far river bank.

A lone swan glides by me
as if to ask my business
then tucks his head into
his beautiful chest to rest.

What in God's name
ever made me think
it would be easier
when you were gone?

The Deer are After the Apples Again

taking their summer pleasure.
They graze beneath the tree outside
my window as though they lived
in a children's petting zoo.

I watch them as I frame
a favorite photo: It's 4:00 a.m.,
I've dressed you in a woolen cap
and heavy parka for the early
morning ride to surgery. No
complaint about the hour, no
grievance with the surgeon,
you smile a cautious smile
as if to show me how a man
should face his death if a man.

The cardinals are stripping
the gooseberry bush as I slide
the image of courage under glass.
It's time to get to work!

The deer are after the apples again.
But how shall we live in the winter?

Counsel

"Crash and burn," anxious pilots
called to each other at take off
during the war, the way actors
bid each other break a leg
on opening night. Well,
it seems our luck's run out.
At last it seems you have spiraled
down in flame without escape.

I've made a little altar for your
dear ashes till we return them
to earth: a photo from the garden,
a wilted rose from the funeral,
an icon of the Blessed Mother.

Friends write and tell me
you stayed on among the stars
like Venus rising in the velvet
blue of summer. I search the sky
looking for you among the fine
needles which pierce the dark.

But you are nowhere to be found,
are lost to me in their cold

brilliance, the infinite sea of light.

This story will not end in joy,
no matter what they say.

Apology

Three years after your husband
jumped from the 102nd floor,
flames licking his heels, I told you
"Enough Betsy, it's time to move on."

I meant it in friendship, with love:
I felt sorry for your pain, wanted
to talk of something other than death
when I got your late-night phone calls.

Well-meaning friends will no doubt
soon hand me back my own words.
"It will take time," they say,
"you will be okay with time."

What is time supposed to do for me,
I wonder? Is it simply a matter of
forgetting you, is that what's expected?
Cleaning the closets of all your hats
and coats and shoes? Putting your photos
into a drawer, your ashes into the vault.

I insist on this pain if letting you drift
into the past is the price I must pay for

happiness. The lessons we learn in life!
How glib you must have thought me
Betsy, when I played Dutch Uncle
and wrapped my tired cliché about
the granite reality of your grief.

Vin Triste

Daisy was first a puppy on this deck,
high over the river. Baby Daisy walked
up to the bucket candles and the light
flickered into her dark eyes like
the magic in the caves of Lascaux.
She never burned her nose, never
caught her chocolate fur on fire. She
was born for this place, claimed it
as her own. And now I walk to the
river, the way we used to do, glass
in hand to watch the fading light of day.

There, swans dot the far bank like
flecks of cotton. Her eyes gone opal
with age, she can not see them, she
bumps into logs and strays from the path.
The mourning doves begin their low,
soft keening. She sits beside me, silky
under my hand, like a weary Oedipus,
trying to understand, searching the river
for you. Neither of us speaks.

I almost can not bear how vision
has taken on the weight of gravity,
every image on the retina a stone,

that simple blade of river grass
pushing through the rock, a sign
of what I must accomplish,
the little dog's blind vigil, true
as the dogs guarding the sleep
of a dead crusader's tomb, the
incriminating light itself, showing
me how often I took your presence
for granted, and simply didn't speak.

"We kept warm together
in cycles of our own turning,"
you wrote once, as the planet
tilted north again. And yes, we did.
You and me and Daisy sat on
the river in firelight, part of it all,
not perfection, but we had those
moments when we were as
much a part of the landscape
as the great oaks holding the river
bank from melting into the ocean
I tip my glass and let the red wine
nourish the earth and your spirit,
a custom from our adopted homeland,
in hopes, that perhaps, it will save us,
and in gratitude.

Gardening

Sunday morning I wake to the sound
of Richie's backhoe extracting the dead
cherry tree that bit like a rotten tooth
into the horizon all winter long,
victim of the evil honeysuckle, your
arch enemy, the 60 years you lived here.

Daisy jumps and barks in the freshly
plowed earth which matches her color
exactly, the excitement of a child on
moving day, a much better game than
licking my nose to rouse me out of bed.

"Coffee, with only cream," Richie calls
from the tractor's cabin and waves,
proud of his neighborly gesture.

"William would have loved
doctoring the trees like this," I tell him,
memory creeping like honeysuckle,
about to choke my heart again, despite
the promise of the freshly tilled earth.
"Ah, he's here all right. He's pruning
over in the secret garden," Richie says,

revving up his engine, blowing off a little black smoke. A slight breeze rises from nowhere, but the day will be blistering.

Maybe, Richie. Maybe he is.

Prayer to Cloacina *

A renter sat where I am sitting
here in the john one winter,
a nurse from the Coast Guard.
Lysol and gardenia permeated
the air with her good husbandry.
In that arctic New England
she ran blue fish, red and
clown-striped fish in a border
atop and under the yellow sea
of the bathroom's walls.

The room smells faintly now
like a urinal. I need, goddess,
a woman in my life.

---

* Cloacina : goddess who presided over the Cloaca Maxima, the system of sewers in Rome. She was also a protector of sexual intercourse in marriage.

Aubade

The gentle deer, lifts one leg
then another, grazing at sunrise
like a puppet on strings. You
could weep for the delicate,
impossible tendons on which
it moves: a cloud, a sunflower
drawn to the sun's slow course.

A humming bird drinks
the hollyhock fountain,
miraculous, in mid-air,
tiny summer rainbow.

If you listen carefully,
you can hear the trees
sing their green joy.

How can I bear this
without you?

Quandary

There is a boy with sandy red hair
making love to me who shoos away
a competitor and suggests that we
drink each other's blood and flesh.

I am driving with people I don't like.
When we get to the end of the road,
the road leads into the ocean, all
is blue water and it is filling the car.
There is no escape and I can not wake.

When you were alive you would have
shaken me and made it clear, even
without words that it was a bad dream,
that I was loved, that I was safe
in the real world of your smile and arms.

What am I to do with no one now
to rouse me from nightmare?

Moot Epiphany

The "grief counselor" is smart
and sweet – Jesus sandals and
a pony tail. Jungian, I suspect.

He says we are a true rarity,
more than simply mates:
two souls that have intertwined,
whose beings have merged and
depend so totally on each the other,
we are one person. My ego flickers
somewhere below consciousness
like a low-battery alarm.

"This is not pathology," he says,
"It can even be seen as something
very glorious. You have taken a
different road, the road less traveled.
But now you see the enormous
price you must pay for who you are."

He hands me my head and
half of my heart with a gentle smile
as I close the office door behind me.

After Berry Picking

The cardinals are pissed,
the blue jays on strike.
The mocking birds speechless,
the humming birds grounded.
Even the bees are a buzz.

I've come like Katrina
to ravish the gooseberry,
thorns and twigs my
late night legacy.

What could I do? Every day
I passed by the rare jewels,
garnet and jade, no security
in sight, ready for the picking.

I slipped on Pink Floyd for a
little distraction, fired up the
barbeque as a smoke screen.

Tonight I'll get out Fannie Farmer
and breakfast on jam and crumpets.
Sorry boys, that's life. I'm a little
angry myself of late. Go make woopy
with some grey thing in the bushes.

Procrastination

Now comes a gentle rain,
drawn like a curtain across
the dusty plot I'd thought
to seed and lime and turn to lawn.
Another missed chance, failed chore:

The gooseberries languish
in the dark fridge like a
saintly host waiting to
sacrifice themselves in a
pot of boiling sugar.

The condolence letters
throb on my desk, the bills
cry out for answer.

The ominous engine light
I've been ignoring all week
burns like a third eye, while I
stare out through the languid rain
in useless, luxurious freedom.

Vortex Ring State

I
The American Caesar isn't concerned:
When your engines start breathing
their own air and you can not "auto rotate,"
(i.e. your flying crucifix becomes a coffin,)
you have only to "get slower and drop."

Without body armor, the boys in Baghdad
will no doubt facilitate this maneuver;
The v-22 Osprey is no Phoenix.

II
My life, it seems, has gone into
Vortex Ring State. I'm descending
into my own downwash, can only
relive the past, without you in my future,
despite my speed, the rate of drop.

"Go to Iceland, visit Japan
Join the Peace Corps in Pango Pango,"
well-meaning friends advise me, when
the most I can seem to manage lately
is watch the deer eat apples,
the hummingbirds tread air.

Mitzvah

Two miles over the maximum
speeding ticket limit last summer
the nice policeman issued instead a
mandatory court date. Great.

I put on a tie and packed a briefcase
full of evidence that I was a
serious person, was not drunk,
couldn't possibly care for you
if you needed the hospital or a doctor
without a car or driver's license.

"Wait here in the hall," I was told and
took my place among the miscreants
of morning, each rehearsing his story.

The clerk's apocalyptic voice rang out
finally down the corridor of doom:
"Richard Harteis approach the bench,"
where the judge sat on high like Moses.

"I want you to know, sir," His Honor began,
"That the long arm of William Meredith has
lifted you up. The world needs more people

like you" - I swear that's what he said, and
I began to cry. "Go take care of your friend
with the gratitude of this court. And don't
forget to give him our best regards."
Dr. Goldberg is slightly charmed
by my story as we begin our session.
I think of how my life changed
the single time my concrete father
stood up for me at school, and how totally
you believed in me all these years, William.
Surrogate father, so what?
You made my life possible.

"His arm would have to be pretty long now,"
Dr. Goldberg says, risking a smile.
It's an amusing comment, I suppose, but,
suddenly once again, I can not breathe.

A Plan

"Richard," you call, waking me
from my first real sleep since
your final sleep and the strange
concoction of codeine dreams.

"What," I say, and you are gone
with hummingbird speed as
the morning comes into focus:
time to feed the dog, seed the
lawn, pack your bags.

A year ago we stood with Yeats
by his grave: "Horseman pass by."
We toured his splendid tower and
Coole Park, where swans keep
their counsel, their beautiful distance,
as do ours, shining on the Thames.

We were at home amid the heroic
rocks of Connemara, brothers to the
granite fields of Connecticut. We walked
the summer of our lives again and were
to return to the land of legend and poetry,
guests of friends who came last spring

to see you through your final hours.

After she died, George Burns, it seems
talked with his wife every day of his life
beyond his hundred years (say good
morning, Gracie) and no one thought him
crazy. So, maybe I'll take you after all.

I never renewed your passport, but
I'll smuggle you in through memory,
illegal immigrant gone underground in
the heart's duress. I'll show you around
through my own eyes - not so blue,
they'll have to do. Take them darling,
they are yours. Perhaps by the time
we reach Ireland, they will be smiling.

Can You Hear Me Now?

Yesterday, top down in the brilliant sun
the cranberry convertible making its way
through the toney Connecticut countryside,
I could not shake your image, collapsed
in the hall, blood streaming from your
dear head to spoil your lemon jacket
and the rest of my life.

"How could I have left him standing,
in my impatience, without a chair, when
I went to park the car," I ask Catherine
who is breaking up on the cell phone
so badly I've missed my turn.

"None of us is superhuman, Richard.
I remember once with Harry, I – crack,
crack – and it was the WAY I said it –
crack – just before he – crack, crack."

And I am breaking up myself now,
the hot, boring tears flow like a
fucking Niagra again to spoil
my shirt and her good intentions .

I close the clamshell shut with a smack
and push on down the road in silence.

Praying with Tammy Faye

Tammy Faye is 65 and weighs 65 pounds.
Asked if she has any life regrets, she tells
the interviewer, "I don't think about it, Larry,
because it's a waste of good brain space."

Some would argue there wasn't
much there to begin with, and
take her in like rubber necking
at a car crash: her ruby blouse
her racoon eyes, already dancing
the danse macabre. Larry's audience
hears the faint tolling of the bell
themselves when it's time to go down
with chicken soup and rice pudding.

"I talk to God every single day," she says,
"and I say, God, my life is in your hands,
and I trust you with me... I believe
when I leave this earth,
because I love the Lord,
I'm going straight to heaven." And
to her fans, "I genuinely love you and
I genuinely care. And I genuinely
want to see you in heaven someday."

The genuine Madonna she may not be,
but I've always loved her pluck, and
when you get there Tammy, say a little prayer
for this sinner please, now (as we leave for
Ireland) and at the hour of my death, Amen.

The Chinese Beech

The Chinese Beech was already
famous nearly 40 years ago when
I first worked this land with you.
It stood like a flagship, anchored
to the river bank, guarding a fleet
of oaks and dogwood, pine and spruce.
There was none greater in the state.
I never thought he'd take it down.

It weathered each season in
grandeur, the primavera leaves
unfolded like a million tiny scrolls
announcing spring for the emperor.
The feathery leaves - no one could
believe it was a beech tree - grew green
and cool against the heat of summer -
in autumn they carpeted the earth
in fiery brilliance, the naked mast
anchored then in the winter sky. Who
could have thought he'd take it down.

It was the reward we offered guests
for a walk to the far end of the garden,
It was the beautiful, the secret prize.

They fingered the delicate leaves in
awe, admired the perfect dimensions:
Platonic notion proclaiming tree – the pride
we took as tangible as friendship.

"I'd like to drift as ashes over the field
and give them that much back," you wrote,
a wish we accorded this spring with friends
under the Chinese beech as it began
it's annual resurrection.

But this is The Year of Magical Thinking:
"We must relinquish the dead, let them go,
keep them dead. Let them become the
photograph on the table. Let them become
the name on the trust accounts. Let go of them
in the water. You have to go with the change."

The new owner came over one afternoon,
if one can speak of owning such a tree,
with his manic saws and tractor like a jolly
serial killer and felled you in an hour. But,
who would have ever thought it possible?
What dark incantation can bring you back?

Flight Crew

He's a nice old codger: bib overalls
and hands like cactus from farming
the good Texas earth after the war.
He regales the flight attendants
hanging like bats from the hand rails
with tales of ship wreck and Jap subs.
His daughter fuels the fire: "Daddy
was the last man out of the water,"
she beams to his admirers.

"I had a friend who flew off carriers
in World War II and Korea...." I often
bragged about you to total strangers
taken by your silver hair, your
Jimmy Stewart good looks and manners.

But the crew is fixed on this live hero
in front of them, heading back to Texas.
"Thank you for your service," one says
respectfully, as we come to the gate.

I'm left standing alone on the flight deck
waiting to flag you in and home
as you make your high, silent way

among the clouds, dreaming poetry,
looking for submarines - a single star,
hanging solitaire in the silver sky
at dusk, at dawn, for eternity now.

Veteran

He clips his cap and sunglasses,
all the paraphernalia of war, to his
nap sack, snug on the mountainous
shoulders. He sports a blond buzz cut,
v waist, granite butt. One pant leg is
folded back into his belt behind him.
He balances on one desert boot and
two aluminum crutches, anchoring him
like the three points of a victorious
jet landing. He smiles, his eyes are blue.
No one on the bus offers him a seat;
everyone is poised to catch him if he falls.
It is as if the proverbial angel has walked
across the room when comes an awkward
silence. He is heartbreakingly beautiful.

He is on a new mission. To forget the
IED's phosphorescent flash, the severed
leg that will not stop itching for a morning run.
Learning to live with the unthinkable, the
constant presence of absence, and carry on.
He's lost his leg and livelihood; I, my love,
and the life I knew. Semper fidelis, brother,
as we step into our future, I salute you.

The Revenant

Daisy stretches herself out like
a mermaid on the kitchen floor.
She throws her head back and wails
for no apparent reason. It could be comic:
Her luxurious cocker ears fall in a chocolate
cascade like the Sun King's wig or a Dutch
Burgomaster. Why so inconsolable, Daisy?

The cookie jar is out of view,
There is no toy you can not reach,
no siren sounds that I can hear. I have
not packed my bags to leave you.

"They look at something we
can't look at yet," you said once
of the ghosts of the house,
"averting their sad glance when
we're clumsy with one another."

Are you playing with us now dear
ghost, tossing an unseen ball to
Daisy, trying to cheer us up a bit?
Does she see you through her
clouded cataracts, the way you

come to me at the edge of sleep?

Do not tease us please, my dear;
Come in full, if apparition. You've
left us lonely beyond measure,
turned Daisy to a banshee, and my
poor brain again, a tree of frantic birds.

A Full Year Come and Gone

Yesterday helicopters filled the sky
like dragon flies, whisking the bods
(nasty local argot for super rich CEO's
and self-righteous celebrities "saving
the world" from their off-shore tax havens,
i.e, got the Celtic tiger by the tail)
back to their offices and swimming pools,
avoiding the traffic jams in Galway
after the world famous horse races.

Today, having done it's bit for the rich
and famous, the sun has gone back to bed,
hiding its head under the sky's grey sheets.
Below, grey bay, grey rocks, grey ponies
by grey walls, whinnying, wistful for an
apple or a kind word, as I jog down the lane
to the harbor. The first year, every day
is an anniversary: these are the same
sweet ponies I took you to meet last year,
just at this moment in summer, our last
summer. I remember more wild flowers
than purple thistle and black bog-rush,
yellow wort and the ruby red fuchsia
called the Tears of God, weeping

with me by the side of the road.

At the dock it seems the tide is out,
I can see the rocks and orange seaweed
below. There's a nice boat with cement
blocks to help it ride the water, and an
old rust bucket called the Radiant II:

You'd like this William: If I threw myself
into the water I'd only get wet or catch
tetanus; I wouldn't make much of a splash
unless I took an anchor with me.

The legend on the lifeguard stand reads,
"A stolen ring buoy is a life stolen."
I leave the life preserver where I find it.
One stolen life is enough for one summer.

Postcard from Achill Island

Dear William, My luggage finally caught up with me and Jack and I drove to Connemara with its "savage beauty," as Oscar Wilde would have it. We stopped for tea at the same pub along the fjord pointing its long, cold finger west through the Pin Mountains to Achill Island. It's barren like Santorini, only green. There are more sheep than people. It rains everyday. Wish you were here. R.

Solitary Confinement

"I write this line in the early morning, before I go off to a round of Freshman English, to remind us both that we are often, if not quite always, together in one another's consciousness. This is a steady joy and strength to me, and even though you know that very well, it's a satisfaction to sit in my vast chilly bedroom here in a westernmost state and write it down. How interesting our lives are, and how much their significance lies in the pattern we weave between them. I am yours dear brother, always, William"

Letter dated 29 September, 1980

How did poet put it,
"Doesn't everything
die at last, and too soon?"

There is nothing outside the universe,
a physicist would tell you, but it seems
at last you have fallen off, my dear,
leaving me with the loneliness
you'd thought to take with you.

I'm all set up now at Heinrich Böll's cottage,
ready to work. I've scones, and jam and butter,
and tea from India. Outside my window,
beyond a curtain of red tears and a field

of purple thistle, the Atlantic dreams on
under the mountains of Achill which
have disappeared in the mist. But I could
as easily be rooming with poor David Fisher,
locked in isolation, dueling with Lucifer:
a tragic Armageddon raging in his
schizophrenic soul — real toads, real garden,
real snakes, real scorpions, the works, that
no amount of Haldol or electro convulsive
therapy will dispel, listening to the "labial
cry of the wolves, "sleeping through winters
of dawn and blue fish." I want to shake him:

"Wake up David, oh, wake up, buddy.
Let your terrors disappear like mist
rising off the mountains. Let's break
out of here honey, let's take the stones
from our chest, and drive up to Big Sur."
But I'm locked in a vast, chilly bedroom
waiting to hear your voice again.
Your consciousness permeates my own
like the air in my lungs, the last breath
I took from you when I kissed you good bye.
But why can't I hear your voice, William,
why can't I hear your voice again?

The Lesson

For John and Maggie

"Have you ever lived alone before,"
John asks, knowing you have died,
solicitous. "Yes," I say, "often alone,
but never lonely...."

No matter the absence, you were
always there at the end of the day
to take me home. Now, I wake
each morning thinking of all the
things we will miss together:
a new president, a new country,
another birthday, another poem.

If there are, in fact, no things,
if all reality is only process, as the
critic said at last night's opening,
then my world now is the frozen
antarctic, I am the jewel-like bug
caught in flight, in a bead of amber.

But if each freckle is the star from
an angel's kiss, then John's face is

a firmament shining down on the
little daughter squirming in his lap.
She's had her chips and ketchup,
and now her sticky hands fly about
like impatient gulls at the beach.

"Is it autism," I ask him, as the little
girl pats my arm and takes me in.
"No, hydrocephalus," he explains,
to yet another well-meaning,
tedious guest. Her hair is braided
with tiny flowers, cornflower blue,
as are her eyes, straying like lost
planets that keep their private,
out-of-kilter orbits. She is so evidently
dear to him. He kisses her and sends
her off to play with the rest of his brood.

I look at the past for a moment
with the child's eyes, and am grateful
for the lesson: I see him and his wife
the first night, as they come home
from the hospital with the angel they
call special. He makes a fire, she
puts on a kettle for tea as they begin
the rest of their life.

Phylactery

They have a season in Ireland
to celebrate Montbritia, a kind of
wild lily, I think, we would call tiger,
that consumes the fields with its fiery
petals throughout the month of August
and by September has disappeared like
the mayfly, come in a day and gone.

But more incredible than the cliffs of Achill,
or the boulders laid by giants along the Atlantic
shore are the ubiquitous red fuchsia the locals
call the Tears of God. Along the lane, at my
gate and window, flowering through the fields,
everywhere you look God is weeping, but
what is He weeping for? Is He weeping for
His Son, who grieves in the garden at midnight,
a son, I make bold to call my brother, about
to face the dark center of life we call death,
the purple core of the flower's red ecstacy.

Only winter will end this vermillion profusion,
only death will end the exhaustion I feel.
I could, like Accurst or your friend John Ferryman,
find a high spot on the cliffs from which to fly,

waving to the passers by as I go down -
There's no kidding myself, I'm doing all the
right things: getting out, exercising, drinking
in moderation — but it's no longer fun without you.
"Friends making off ahead of time on their own,"
you called "wilful," a "dread recidivism." I know
you would not approve. So, I wait dutifully
on the shore till winter come and end this
endless red weeping in hope that after,
may come reunion and tears of joy.

Make me Your phylactery Father, render me
Your vessel, until, with John, I am able to cry,
"Fantastic! Fantastic! Thank Thee dear Lord."

Symbiosis

When my dreams molt into
nightmare lately, so it seems,
do yours. It's the tone of your
voice that wakes me, the way
you cried, "pain, pain," as you
woke from surgery last winter.

Then it was a good thing.
It meant you had survived,
were coming back to life.

What can it mean now,
calling to me like that
from the other side of death?

You stand like a lifeguard
in the mirror, warning me
of dark shapes in the water,
the channel widening as I swim.

Do you dream of me in death,
as I do you in life? Have you
claimed my pain as your own,
as I do yours? Can I kill the beast

in your dream by waking, and if
you live but in dream what then?

Where am I, where are we
in this strange ether. I can not
sleep, I can not sleep, darling.
Or are we only dreaming?

Day Tripper

I
The boatman's young, the picture of Irish youth:
ginger hair and apple cheeks flecked with freckles.
He keeps an easy hand on the wheel, a casual
eye on the heavy swells as we bob past
Croag Patrick, the "Holy Mountain" where, the saint,
they say, banished Ireland's snakes into the sea.

"And they all swam to the states and became
policemen and prison guards, according to
Jim Larkin, cooling his heels in Sing Sing."

Our host, Dr. King, is on call, a garrulous guide:
has the gift of gab, as well as healing as we sail
on Clew Bay to Clare Island to make his weekly
rounds. Everything arrives by boat here,
from compassion to tinned goods, including a few
friends and tourists he's brought along for the ride:
the French boys who won last week's fishing competition,
his sister Katherine and his small niece, Clonah,
a visiting priest who might come in handy, and the
sad sack poet who could use, it seems, a little fresh air.

They share custard creams and chocolate as they

hike the lane along the sea up to the ancient abbey
where Grace O'Malley, the pirate queen lies buried. Aloof
heifers sport yellow tags like costly ear rings and feign an
interest as we pass by. A lone donkey stands immobile in the
field, lost in some private reverie. The day-glow sheep, marked
with their owner's unique rainbow, take their non-stop lunch,
insouciant. Only a shepherd puppy jumps out with pleasure,
and pees us a greeting.

When the cookies run out, Katherine teaches her
little daughter how to suck the Fuchsia blossoms
for a drop of honey. She lacks the humming bird's
skill, her lips have gone cherry from drinking the
sweet ambrosia in the purple stems of "God's Tears."

II
Were you with us, William, you'd have loved
the feisty Queen's resting place. No saints for
"Bald Grace": the ceiling in her chapel sports knights in mail
armor for company, hot wolves after a stag, a dragon in need
of slaying. But, I'm not sure she would be happy with the
cemetery that has grown up about her like a carnival on the
beach for children.

Oh, there are a few ancient crosses worn by
wind and weather to a noble anonymity. But

mostly it's a sentimental statuary, a field of
angels, weeping Madonnas, and multiple
Jesus' all pointing to a sacred, radiating heart.
The beds in which the dead lie are a riot
of sea glass, green and aquamarine –
over-the- top marble and sentiment – but,
who can blame the sad relatives for turning
death into a little Miami when winter comes
to ruin their life. It's contagious, this need
to see leprechauns in Ireland, to ask if it's you,
in fact, William, coming down that ladder of light
that breaks through the black sky like alchemy
turning the sea into a lake of gold as we make
our tired way home. I don't have any answers
fancier than the Irish sister who sent her man
off in stone so simply on the island of Clare:

"Looking back with memories
upon the path you trod
the days we had with you
and give you back to God."

MacDowell Colony - Ireland West

For Violet

You'd like Mrs. MacDowell, William,
the widow down the lane who runs
Gray's Hotel and lets me ring Dublin
to collect my email. She treated me
to a glass of wine the other night as
she held court in her salon, clad in
pink suede and lavender silk like
the improbable lilies in her garden.
A local bard wrote a poem for her
in 2000 as she turned 90 - Age,
she would tell you, is only a number.

Nobody wears a watch at Gray's
they follow the natural rhythms from
soup to sherry to conversation around
the fire, blue smoke rising sweet from
the peat, licked by the flame's orange
tongue, under the watchful eye of her
cousins the Sheridans, in powdered
wigs and theatrical get up - pink and
lavender, and her husband, chatting
amiably with her grandfather on the

opposite wall in a photo twice her age,
No teetotalers here and all the spirits
are welcome in her parlor.

She's one of the "radical old" you
admired, "who persist in being at
home in the world, who just naturally
feel it is a good bind to be in." And
She's got nice friends like Bernie,
confident as a fox as he complains
that he can't hear the punch lines
in my poems. "I do it for effect,"
I tell him. "Well, your WRONG,"
he says. I love it.

Remember you said you wouldn't
go "upstairs" until you were 102?
You checked out far too early William.
Come sit for a while with us darling.
Mrs. MacDowell is serving tea and sweets,
and outside, the night has grown far too dark.

Spiderman

One night you told me you were dying.
"No honey, you're not dying," I lied.
"I'm going to take you home. We've built
a sidewalk and we can take your wheelchair
down to the terrace. Daisy misses you."

The hypnotic hours drifted into days,
then weeks, the numbing monotony
of death. Night after night I slept
by your side, the classical music
playing from the radio I'd bought
to entertain you non-stop and help
us sleep. I lay tangled in your dream
catcher, and each morning the idiot
white coats swept in like the Sand Man
with clipboards and stethoscopes
and little else by way of hope. I thought
maybe I'd be a better visitor if I got out
for a while and went to see the movie
the whole world was talking about.

All winter long they waited for Spiderman
to save them from the doldrums, banish
boredom, return them to the joys of childhood.
Spidey mania swept round the world like

checkerboard meridians encircling the globe:
Spiderman cups, and caps, and credit cards,
Spiderman at the supermarket, Spiderman
at the gas pump. But with spring, the critics
said, came one of Hollywood's more odious
stink bombs: In like a lion, out like a lamb.
A creature from an evil star, an improbable
deus ex machina in the form of a black goo
takes Spidey over and turns him into his worst self.
We are not talking Sophocles here, no amount
of canned applause or ooo's or ah's from the masses
while our hero battles his alter ego and the heroine
dangles 80 floors above the streets will save the day.

Now as I fly back home over the Atlantic, I get
the chance finally to see Spiderman in action.
The movie's not too old yet, nor the pain.
I find an empty seat to think it through.
How could I have seen it when you were
dying? It's unbearable now, weeks later.

Spidey says good bye to his best friend who
dies in technicolor green at the end. He gets
the girl, they hold hands and look dreamily into
the sunrise symbolizing their bright future as
Mr. and Mrs. Spiderman.

"Throw me a line Spiderman," I want to cry,
"Save me super hero. I'm falling from the sky
and there's no one here to catch me."

But it's the same old story. How can I ask
starry-eyed Spiderman to rescue me
any more than he could save his friend,
any more than I could save mine.

Legacy

People loved your blue eyes
your crooked smile. The nurses
puzzled over your biceps, rock
hard from transplanting trees.
These were the spirit's tools -
love, compassion, strength
and courage becoming flesh.

As a man will inherit a strong back
blond hair, or a gentle disposition,
The end to grief may lie within'
a private transformation:
to let your spirit work in me
so that if I am kind for your sake,
in your memory, if I remember
how sweetly you dealt with others
and model myself on that civility,
if I stand against injustice, bigotry
or hatred as you did, then your life
goes on in me, your death no longer
meaningless, your death no longer
death, at least while I live or
this poem, the well will be
replenished, my small steps join
the tribe's slow progress.

Richard Harteis is a poet, fiction writer and translator. His most recent publications include a novel, SAPPHIRE DAWN, a new and selected poems, PROVENCE, and the re-issue of a non-fiction work first published by W.W. Norton in 1989 entitled MARATHON. All three works are available through Vivisphere Books (www.Vivisphere.com). He lives in Uncasville, Connecticut.

www.ingramcontent.com/pod-product-compliance
Lightning Source LLC
Chambersburg PA
CBHW021025090426
42738CB00007B/905